48 CASE STUDIES

48 CASE STUDIES

EQUIPPING CHRISTIANS FOR DISCIPLESHIP

RICK THOMAS

48 CASE STUDIES:
Equipping Christians for Discipleship

ISBN 978-1-966741-15-2

Rick Thomas

Edited by Sheron Wallace

Life Over Coffee
8595 Pelham Rd Ste 400 #406,
Greenville, SC 29615
LifeOverCoffee.com

Dedication

To my Mastermind Students

For additional resources, visit
lifeovercoffee.com

Table of Contents

Introduction

Our all-online Mastermind training course equips Christians to become compassionate and competent disciple-makers. The program has three parts. The foundational piece is theology—the study of God. What we know about and how we think about the Almighty is the bedrock upon which we build our Christian lives. Theologically precise Christians can live well in God's world, but they need more than theology. Bible knowledge can provide an orthodoxy with a deficient orthopraxy (practice), which is why our students receive more than sound theological training.

We teach them psychology, too. Psychology is "psyche logos," or the "study of the soul," or the "Word concerning the soul." We call this sanctification—the practical application of theology to our everyday lives. Our students must know how to connect God's Word—the psychology book—to their souls and those they serve. Most biblical counseling training is academic and theoretical. There is little "original knowledge," which is taking "classical knowledge" (God's Word) and contextualizing it in real-world relationships and situations. Thus, we provide our students with theology and biblical psychology, with an emphasis on practical application. We must be more than theorists.

Too often, discipleship training does not get into the nuts and bolts of our real lives, making the third phase of our

Mastermind training essential. We want our students to add to their studies of God and humanity. We require them to make it practical by applying their training to everyday situations. In real estate, it's about location, location, location. At Life Over Coffee, it's about application, application, application. We help our students do this in several ways, one of which is our case study training manual. Throughout their Mastermind Program, we require each student to complete one case study for every block of assignments. There are forty-eight blocks altogether. The case studies are approximately 250 words, and there are two to five questions for them to answer for each fictional scenario.

This book has all forty-eight case studies. (The expanded version has the leader notes, which are our analysis of the forty-eight case studies.) We ask our students to write a comprehensive response about how they might counsel each situation. Once submitted, we challenge them on what they said.

This book is an excellent training tool for the Christian discipler. It is perfect for small group discussions. (The expanded version provides leader notes and practical details to assist the trainer.) This book is also ideal for counselor training because it will challenge the student to go beyond counseling theory. The hardest part of our program is, without question, these case studies. Christians enjoy reading about theology and counseling theory. They love gaining knowledge from so many terrific authors— as they should. But when it comes to doing the work of discipleship while relying on the Spirit and His Word, the level of difficulty increases exponentially as it involves the application of God's Word.

We want our students to have more than fantastic Christian knowledge and a theoretical understanding of life. We want them to know how to apply their theology to real lives. These case studies help accomplish that goal.

If you think you might be interested in our Mastermind Program, please get in touch with us at Life Over Coffee. It would be a pleasure to explore that possibility with you. As you are thinking about that option, please share our case studies with your friends. Engage your friends. Talk about how you'd counsel the individuals, couples, families, and situations presented in this manual.

My professor, Stuart Scott, said, "Wisdom is knowledge applied." May you continue to grow in the knowledge of God's Word, and may your skill at applying it practically into your life and your friends grow proportionally.

Rick

Case 1

Procrastination

Mable is a highly successful woman who has achieved much in her career and personal life. She is married to Biff, and together, they share a strong faith and a stable marriage. However, despite her many accomplishments, Mable struggles with persistent procrastination, particularly when it comes to tasks that require personal discipline or have less accountability. This recurring problem has caused tension in her marriage and added stress to her daily life.

Mable describes her procrastination as an ongoing frustration. She acknowledges that she often delays tasks until the last moment, creating unnecessary pressure for herself and others. While she thrives in more structured environments and enjoys the recognition that comes from achieving goals, she struggles with smaller, less glamorous tasks, often putting them off until they become urgent.

While supportive, Biff has expressed concerns about how Mable's procrastination affects their relationship. He feels that her delays often place additional stress on him, as he must adjust to accommodate her last-minute efforts to meet deadlines. Though he loves her deeply, this dynamic has introduced a recurring tension in their otherwise healthy marriage.

Mable is seeking counsel to address this issue. She wants to understand why she excels in some areas while struggling in others and how she can overcome procrastination in a way that aligns with her faith and strengthens her marriage.

Case Study Questions

1. Where would you begin in counseling Mable about her procrastination?
2. What questions would you ask Biff to understand how this affects their marriage?
3. Why do you think Mable excels in some areas but struggles in others?
4. What ruling motives of her heart might be contributing to her procrastination?
5. How would you guide her to address these heart issues biblically?

Case 2

To Date or Not to Date

Biffina is 18 years old, the oldest of four children in a close-knit Christian family. Her parents, Biff and Mable, have consistently taught their children God's Word and modeled it faithfully. The children have embraced their parents' teaching, and no significant issues have arisen within the family.

One of the principles Biff has emphasized is that dating should only happen when his children are ready for marriage and when a suitable person comes along. He understood how assessments are subjective, hence the concern. His preference was that dating would only occur after college. This teaching was well-received, and all the children initially agreed with it.

Now, in her first semester at the local university, Biffina has approached her father to share that she wants to date and has already started seeing a boy on campus. This new development has left Biff and Mable trying to figure out how to respond. They want to respect her independence as an adult but are hesitant because of their strong preference against dating at this stage in her life.

Biff and Mable come to you seeking advice on how to navigate this situation biblically. They want to know how to maintain a godly influence while allowing their daughter the freedom to make her own decisions.

Case Study Questions

1. Is it wrong for Biffina to date? Why or why not?
2. What does honoring her parents look like now that she is living outside their home?
3. What Scriptures would you use to guide the parents in this situation?
4. If Biffina sought counsel, how would you guide her?

Case 3

Exchanging Prisons

Mable, at 28, was single and deeply desired marriage. She had a degree, a great job, and a seemingly full life, but she felt an emptiness that she attributed to her singleness. Marriage, in her mind, was the next milestone she longed to achieve. You might say that Mable was the epitome of a goal-oriented lady.

Although she assured her friends that she was not desperate, her thoughts and conversations often revolved around marriage. Scriptures about peace, contentment, loneliness, and God-fulfilling desires intertwined in her heart confusingly and subjectively, leaving her discouraged and impatient.

Eventually, Mable married Biff, believing he was the answer to her prayers. He seemed like a kind, godly man. However, after a year of marriage, Mable felt trapped, describing her situation as a "prison switch." She traded the prison of singleness for what now felt like a never-ending, hopeless marriage. Additionally, Biff's hidden sins surfaced early in their marriage:

1.   Fear of others
2.   Hypocrisy
3.   Flirtatious behavior
4.   Financial debt
5.   Pornography
6.   Materialism
7.   A lack of close friends

Mable feels overwhelmed by her circumstances, uncertain of how to move forward in a marriage she cannot escape.

Case Study Questions

1. What is Mable's core sin issue? Why did you say that?
2. How would you offer Mable hope?
3. She can't divorce Biff, so how would you help her practically?
4. If you had an opportunity to guide her pastor, what would you tell him?

Case 4

The Nagging Wife

Mable has struggled with insecurity her entire life. Her earliest memories involve her parents' consistent displeasure with her, valuing her outward appearance in social contexts over her well-being. This fear-driven parenting model shaped Mable's need to prove herself and escape the feelings of inadequacy instilled by her parents. After you toss in Adamic shame, it was a crippling double-whammy.

One of Mable's coping mechanisms became criticizing others. Whether verbal or internal, judging others as inferior provided her with a sense of self-righteous superiority and temporary relief from her feelings of inadequacy.

When Biff married Mable, he recognized her insecurity but overlooked it due to her physical attractiveness and perceived virtues. Within two years of marriage, however, Biff realized he could not satisfy Mable's expectations, leading to his sinful pursuits to seek significance and acceptance elsewhere.

Now, Biff is searching for help for his actions, and the counselor is aware of Mable's deep-seated battles with insecurity. The challenge lies in approaching Mable to address her critical spirit and how her nagging has contributed to the strain in their marriage. While Biff is fully responsible for his sins, Mable must confront her patterns to bring lasting transformation to their relationship.

Case Study Questions

1. How and why would you approach Mable?
2. What are Mable's core problems and solutions?
3. How would a right understanding and application of the gospel radically change their marriage?

Case 5

Suicide

Mable picked up the phone and started calling people at random. Somehow, she ended up with your number. Mable confessed she didn't know why she was calling you but felt an inexplicable urge to do so. She began to share her sordid story: she was at the end of a complicated and frustrating life and felt hopeless.

Mable explained that she had "tried God," but in her words, "He didn't work for me." Admittedly, as you inquired more, she did reveal her lack of understanding of Christianity. She talked about how she had mapped out her plans for death the previous week, written goodbye notes, and tied up loose ends. She believed there was nothing left to do but end her life. Yet, before taking that final step, she felt compelled to make one more phone call—and you answered.

Mable is a divorced Christian and the mother of a teenager. She attends a Southern Baptist church but lacks strong connections within the community. Her church has not been intentional about building relationships with her, which was great for Mable because her default was to isolate. She hasn't maintained a job for the past 15 years due to a diagnosis and the prescribed medications. Now middle-aged, lonely, fearful, and weary, she is nervous and overwhelmed by despair. "What's the use?" she asks.

Case Study Questions

1. What else would you like to know about Mable?
2. What kind of detailed plan would you map out to help her? Be practical.
3. Based on the information that you currently have, how do you think Mable got to the point where she wants to take her life?

Case 6

Counseling the Un-counsel-able

Mable presented herself as an ideal counselee: open, honest, and seemingly eager for change. In your first session, she shared her struggles with remarkable transparency, leaving no detail uncovered. Her vulnerability moved you, and her apparent willingness to receive correction quickly filled you with hope for genuine transformation.

However, as the weeks progress, a troubling pattern emerges. Each session circles back to the same exhaustive list of complaints. Despite your biblical counsel and her verbal acknowledgment of its value, no meaningful progress is evident. It becomes clear that Mable has idolized her suffering, finding comfort in the attention and sympathy garnered from recounting her problems to you.

As her counselor, your initial compassion begins to erode. Frustration, cynicism, and even anger creep in, overshadowing your desire to minister effectively. Instead of seeing Mable as a soul in need of truth and grace, you start viewing her as a burden. Your patience diminishes as the repetitive cycle continues, and you sense that your hope in God's transformative power in her life is being replaced by a desire to confront her directly and disengage from the relationship altogether.

This case raises critical questions about how to navigate a counselor's heart response and maintain faithfulness in ministering to the unresponsive counselee.

Case Study Questions

1. What could be going on in the heart of the counselor?
2. How would you counsel the counselor about the lack of compassion for Mable?
3. How would you practically walk the counselor through this sin problem?

Case 7

When Prayer Kills a Church

Biff is an angry man whose temper has caused significant issues in his marriage. Two weeks ago, Mable gave him an ultimatum: seek help or face the end of their marriage. In response, Biff reluctantly attended church with Mable last Sunday—the first time in over 11 years.

Mable's church is a solid, God-loving, conservative community with authentic relationships and a deep affection for Christ. However, Biff found the experience deeply uncomfortable. During the worship service, he was unsettled by the congregants lifting their hands in praise. Before the sermon, the pastor invited the congregation to gather in small groups for prayer, making it clear that their participation was optional.

When it was Biff's turn to pray, he felt humiliated, angry, and judged by the strangers in his group. The experience left him feeling alienated rather than welcomed by them, which heightened his resistance to ever going back. Now, Mable faces a challenging situation. She wants to honor God in her marriage but doesn't know how to navigate Biff's reaction. Additionally, the pastor, noticing Biff's discomfort, asked Mable about her husband's response to the service, leaving her unsure how to proceed in helping Biff without driving him further away.

Case Study Questions

1. Should the church people seek to be who they are unashamedly, or should they be more attentive to the seeker's expectations? Explain your answer.
2. The pastor asked Mable about Biff's response to the church meeting. What would you tell him if you were Mable?
3. What are the pros of the seeker-sensitive movement?
4. What are the cons to the seeker-sensitive movement?

Case 8

When Thin Is In

Mable is consumed with her appearance, weight, and food choices. She frequently fasts, not out of a heartfelt desire to glorify God with her body or soul, but as a means to control her image and find approval. Contradictions mark her conversations—she often projects self-righteousness in her discipline yet also reveals deep insecurity through her comparisons to others.

Though Mable claims her actions are part of her pursuit of God, her behaviors suggest misplaced priorities and underlying idolatries. She seems to tie identity and value to more external appearances and self-control rather than to her standing as a child of God. These patterns have left her struggling with dissatisfaction, fear, and an inability to rest in God's provision and love.

Mable's interactions with others often revolve around her achievements in dieting and self-discipline; she subtly uses these tactics to gain approval from or superiority over others. Yet, her self-critical thoughts and comparisons reveal the exhausting burden she carries in seeking peer affirmation through fleeting and superficial means. She longs for a true sense of purpose and value but has misplaced her pursuit of controlling what she can see rather than trusting in God's unchanging grace. Exhausted, she finally gives in and comes to you for counseling, hoping to break the cycle of self-love.

Case Study Questions

1. What is Mable's core heart issue, and why do you believe this?
2. What aspects of the gospel is she missing, and how would you present them?
3. What questions would you ask to uncover deeper motivations behind her behaviors?
4. Prioritize her idols (self-righteousness, control, comfort, guilt, and fear) and explain why you ordered them that way.

Case 9

Are You Certified?

Biff and Mable have been married for 17 years, but their covenant relationship has been fraught with challenges for much of that time. They have two teenage sons who are nearing adulthood, and the prospect of an empty nest leaves Mable filled with dread. As she considers her future, she realizes she knows very little about Biff, and what she does know discourages her.

Desperate for help, Mable approached her pastor for guidance. However, he admitted he did not feel equipped to address the complexities of their marital struggles and advised her to seek a local Christian counselor. Following his suggestion, Mable began a search online for a biblical counselor. In her search, Mable came across your social media platform, which highlights your Christian counseling services. She emailed you, briefly outlining her marital challenges. She wrapped up with this question: "Are you certified?"

Mable's question reflects her desire for assurance that the counselor she chooses is both competent and aligned with practical biblical principles. Her inquiry reveals her need for confidence as she navigates the sensitive and complex task of addressing long-standing issues in her marriage. Mable's priority is finding someone she can trust to provide biblical wisdom and practical support.

Case Study Questions

1. You respond to her with a "yes" or "no," depending on whether or not you are certified. Based on your reply, what else would you say to encourage her to come to you for counseling?
2. What does certification by a legit biblical counseling organization mean? Is it necessary to be certified? Why or why not?
3. What is the difference between a Christian counselor who is certified and one who is not?
4. Are you certified or not? If not, will you become certified? Please explain your answers.

Case 10

An Anxious Need to Be Right

Mable is a perfectionist driven by an anxious need to be right. She holds herself and others to impossible standards, striving to present a carefully edited image she believes will earn acceptance, significance, and admiration. Mable's fear of being wrong fuels a pattern of self-righteous criticism, blame-shifting, and rationalization. These behaviors help her deflect attention from her shortcomings and maintain control over how others perceive her.

In social situations, Mable tends to stay quiet unless she is confident she can meet her self-imposed expectations, which limits her ability to connect meaningfully with others. Her controlling tendencies, combined with a self-righteous fear of being wrong, make it difficult for her to engage in constructive dialogue. Consequently, she has only a few close friends and struggles in her relationships.

Mable's craving for control has created significant strain in her marriage. Feeling overwhelmed and isolated, her husband struggles to communicate with her and often avoids confrontation to maintain peace. He is desperate for guidance on how to support Mable while navigating his own frustrations and spiritual exhaustion. Understanding her need for approval and fear of failure is key to helping her recognize her patterns and pursue transformation.

Case Study Questions

1. What would you tell Mable's husband initially?
2. What would be your plan to walk him through what he needs to do to help Mable?

Case 11

Don't Tell Anyone I'm in Counseling

Mable sought counseling with a specific request: under no circumstances should her pastor find out. Her insistence on anonymity is common among Christians today.

Historically, pastors were the primary caregivers for their congregations, walking closely with their people through trials and difficulties. However, in the modern church, many Christians, like Mable, prefer to seek help outside their local churches, turning to parachurch ministries or independent counselors for assistance.

While parachurch organizations and counselors can offer valuable short-term care, God never intended for them to replace the long-term shepherding and accountability that only a local church can provide. Mable, like every believer, will face ongoing struggles with sin and suffering—outside of the counseling season—that require enduring spiritual care. God's design for this sanctifying process is a person's family and their local church, where relationships are built on love, truth, and mutual accountability, all under the leadership of shepherds who care for their souls.

The challenge in counseling Mable is to respect her desires while helping her see and value her church as God's provision for her long-term sanctification and care.

Case Study Questions

1. Would you counsel Mable? Why or why not?
2. Would you try to give her a vision for the local church as the long-term solution for care? Why or why not? How would you do it?
3. Do you believe the local church is God's answer for the sanctification needs of His people? Please explain.

Case 12

I Want Out of This Marriage!

Mable contacted a Christian counselor to address her dissatisfaction with her marriage. During her initial session, she made it clear that she wanted to leave her husband. She rationalized that their marriage had become unfulfilling after seven years, and she longed for the satisfaction and joy she felt when they first met and believed that she deserved it.

Over several sessions, Mable seemed to make progress. She began applying biblical principles to her life, and her outlook on her circumstances started to improve. However, there was a sticking point: her heart toward her husband remained unchanged, and true reconciliation did not occur. Eventually, Mable followed through with her original plan to divorce her husband. She secured a job, rebuilt her life, and enjoyed the initial "honeymoon phase" of her new independence. For a time, she felt relief and satisfaction in her new lifestyle.

As the years passed, however, Mable found herself back in a familiar place of emptiness and discontentment. The relief she had felt faded, and she began to experience the same dissatisfaction that plagued her in her marriage. She contacted her counselor again, seeking help to understand why she remained unfulfilled despite having the life she thought she wanted.

I Want Out of This Marriage!

Case Study Questions

1. Where would you begin with Mable? What questions would you ask?
2. What do you think Mable is interpreting as her needs? Why do you believe this?
3. What Scriptures would you use to help Mable see her real problem?

37

Case 13

He Cannot Lead His Wife

Biff and Mable have sought biblical counseling after transitioning to their new church, following a recommendation from their previous pastor. The pastor noted Biff's struggle to lead his wife, a concern that became evident during your first session.

In the session, Mable dominated the entire conversation, frequently answering questions for Biff and controlling their interactions. Her assertiveness contrasts sharply with Biff's passivity. He avoids potential conflict, disengages from discussions, and increasingly spends less time at home, creating further distance in their relationship.

The dynamics of their marriage reveal a significant imbalance. Mable has taken over the leadership role that biblically belongs to Biff while he retreats from his God-given responsibilities. Both spouses are caught in a cycle of frustration—Mable compensates for her husband's lack of initiative, and Biff withdraws further under the weight of her controlling tendencies.

Their entrenched habits and relational imbalances present challenges to restoring biblical order in their marriage. While they desire clarity and help, these patterns complicate efforts to foster mutual respect and establish a marriage where both partners fulfill their roles in a way that honors God.

Case Study Questions

1. In this first session, who should be your primary focus, and why?
2. How would you establish structure and balance for the next few sessions?
3. What biblical principles would you use to help Biff take responsibility for his role?
4. How would you counsel Mable to honor her husband's leadership biblically?
5. What strategies would you use to maintain order in your counseling sessions?

Case 14

I Don't Know What to Do with My Life

Biff, a 24-year-old, has cycled through seven jobs in five years and is currently unemployed. His pattern of chasing big plans and get-rich-quick schemes every few months reflects his passion for starting projects but a lack of discipline to see them through. While Biff's charm and likability have endeared him to many, his growing reputation for being unreliable is causing friends and job opportunities to slip away.

Though outwardly upbeat, Biff's weariness is evident. The strain of his constant restarts has taken a toll on him, leaving him spiritually and physically drained. His friends are transient, as old friends begin to distance themselves after witnessing his lack of follow-through and consistency. With nobody close to him, there isn't anyone to hold him accountable or dare speak into his life.

Biff also struggles with debt, being overweight, and a persistent sense of discouragement. Lacking motivation and an ability to handle details, he finds himself stuck in a constant state of flux. Despite seeing four counselors before seeking your help, Biff still feels lost and uncertain about his life's direction. His primary goal is to find clarity and figure out what to do with his life. At the same time, you recognize the deeper need to address his heart issues and underlying motivations for lasting transformation.

Case Study Questions

1. What else would you like to know about Biff?
   Where would you start?
2. What behavioral homework assignments would you
   give him?
3. Name three possible "heart idols." Why would you
   say that?

Case 15

Don't Tell the Elders

Biff, a 32-year-old aspiring pastor, has anchored his identity in ministry rather than in Christ. His parents have perpetuated this mindset with a two-tier Christian belief system that elevates ministry work above other vocations. This perspective has driven Biff's pursuit of pastoral leadership, even though his marriage with Mable is fraught with unresolved challenges.

Mable resents the pressures of ministry life, especially the "fishbowl" effect of living under constant surveillance. Their most heated arguments consistently revolve around Biff's ministry ambitions. Recently, Mable expressed her unwavering stance: she will not divorce Biff, but she will also never support his desire to become a pastor.

Biff is torn between his aspirations for ministry and the mounting tension in their marriage. He knows the two cannot coexist in their current state but fears losing his ministry position if the elders discover the truth about his marriage struggles. This fear of transparency intensifies his internal conflict, creating uncertainty about the next steps. Biff must face the reality that his ministry cannot thrive if his marriage is not aligned with biblical qualifications for leadership. He seeks guidance on reconciling his calling, the state of his marriage, and his commitment to living with integrity.

Case Study Questions

1. Why do you believe Biff should (or should not) be in the ministry?
2. What Scriptures would you use to counsel Biff, and why would you use them?
3. What should their marriage look like for him to be qualified for the ministry?

Case 16

You Need to Please God

Mable struggles with the fear of man, often described as people-pleasing or codependency. Her functional theology is performance-driven, centering on earning approval from others rather than resting in Christ's finished work. This exhausting lifestyle has left her broken and ready for change. While she is a believer, her faith feels more burdensome than joyful.

When Mable sought help from a biblical counselor, the counselor correctly identified her primary issue as the fear of man. The counselor encouraged her to shift her focus to God's opinion of her and to prioritize pleasing Him over others. This advice was liberating for Mable, who was weary of living under the control of others' expectations. With a renewed sense of hope, Mable began the counselor's suggestions. She started reading two books, set aside time for daily journaling, and increased her prayer time.

Despite initial optimism, Mable felt overwhelmed and anxious within two weeks. She struggled to maintain the disciplines while managing her other responsibilities, and her inability to do so led to fears that God was displeased with her. Mable returned to her counselor, expressing her frustration and concern. She felt trapped between the expectations of others and the pressures she had placed on herself to meet God's standards.

Case Study Questions

1. Where did the counselor go wrong?
2. If you were counseling Mable, how would you approach her situation?
3. What does the counselor's advice to Mable reveal about the counselor's theology and practice?
4. What five assignments would you give her to help her overcome the fear of others? Make three assignments short-term and the other two long-term.

Case 17

Cheap Plates Overcome Anger

Biff sought counseling for his anger and shared that his previous counselor suggested buying cheap plates to throw into the fireplace whenever he felt anger rising. Biff explained that the sound, the aim, and the shattering effect temporarily helped him vent his anger. The advice stemmed from the psychologist's belief that anger operates like a hydraulic system: pressure builds inside, and releasing it prevents an "emotional explosion." To validate the theory, the psychologist used phrases:

- "I was boiling mad."
- "You just need to let off steam."
- "I have to get away, or I'm going to explode."

Unfortunately, these metaphors were not just descriptors of feelings but were used to diagnose the problem, albeit inaccurately. If this idea were true, Biff's metaphorical pressure would diminish with every shattered plate, but the pattern continued, revealing that venting didn't address the heart of Biff's issue. The truth is that his anger was not an uncontrollable force victimizing him. It was a habitual sin response stemming from fear and a refusal to trust God at the moment. Anger seeks to manipulate circumstances and people back into a more comfortable and ordered state for the raging soul.

Case Study Questions

1. What is your theology of anger?
2. Write a detailed plan to help Biff overcome his problem.

Case 18

I Will Forgive But Never Forget

Mable has endured the pain of her husband Biff's infidelity. After months of counseling and repentance, Biff has committed to restoring his relationships with Mable, the Lord, and their children. Although not perfect, Biff has shown consistent effort and progressive change, demonstrating genuine repentance.

Mable insists that she has forgiven Biff and states that his adultery is behind them. However, her observed behavior tells another story. Her subtle anger manifests as critical, condemning, and judgmental attitudes toward Biff. When confronted, she becomes defensive, adamantly declaring, "I have forgiven him, but I will never forget what he and others have done to me!"

Her insistence on forgiveness, paired with persistent bitterness, reveals an unresolved struggle in her heart. While her words claim forgiveness, her attitudes suggest she is either unaware of or unwilling to acknowledge the ongoing effects of resentment and unforgiveness in her life. Mable's bitterness not only strains their marriage but also hinders her spiritual growth, as her heart remains tethered to the offenses of the past. Addressing this issue requires a careful balance of compassion and truth, helping her see how biblical forgiveness leads to freedom and restoration.

Case Study Questions

1. Where would you start with Mable?
2. What is your counsel to a person who forgives but does not forget?
3. Which do you think she is: self-deceived or willfully lying about her sin? Why did you answer that way?
4. How can Biff help Mable through her sinful attitudes?

Case 19

The Fearful Parent

Biff, a Certified Nutritionist and devoted father, is navigating the complexities of parenting children with a disease that suppresses their immune systems. While the children show no symptoms, Biff is highly aware that the bacteria in their bodies thrive on refined sugar. Determined to protect their health, he strictly avoids allowing his kids to consume sugar but occasionally compromises in social settings, leaving him overwhelmed with guilt and fear.

This fear of harm has led Biff to avoid all social events, believing it is the way to effectively control his children's diet. Both Biff and Mable are deeply committed to raising their children in a manner that honors the Lord. However, they struggle to balance their responsibility as parents with a proper biblical understanding of God's sovereignty.

They often find themselves wrestling with the tension between their trust in God and the practical challenges of managing their children's health. Seeking biblical counsel, Biff and Mable hope to receive guidance on how to parent faithfully while addressing their fears. They desire a way forward that allows them to trust the good Lord's care without compromising their responsibility to protect their children's well-being.

Case Study Questions

1. Biff wants to know if he should violate his conscience and feed his kids any sugar because God is sovereign and controls all things. How would you counsel him?
2. How would you walk Biff through the fear-related issues regarding his unwillingness to attend social functions where his kids can eat the wrong foods?
3. What do you think is Biff's core issue? What main thing would you want to help Biff to see?

Case 20

If I Tell the Truth, They Will Expel Me

Biff, a rising junior at a local Christian college, is struggling with pornography and masturbation. These temptations began when he was 12 years old, introduced to him by a friend. At the time, Biff found it strange but stimulating, though he was unaware of the addictive nature of what his friend encouraged him to do.

Biff's upbringing was marked by a strained relationship with his father, an insecure, angry, and harsh man. Over the years, their relationship deteriorated, leading Biff to give up on pursuing a meaningful connection. This void of relationship contributed to his deep fear of man and desire for affirmation.

Pornography became Biff's means of escape, offering a virtual, no-risk way to experience intimacy while avoiding the pain of rejection. While it satisfied his physical desires temporarily, it left him trapped in a cycle of shame, guilt, and regret. Biff is a Christian who despises living a double life and wants to change. However, his college enforces a strict demerit-to-expulsion policy. He does not want to delay his education but finds rehabilitation unreachable, which fills him with fear and uncertainty.

Now, Biff seeks guidance on whether to confess his struggles to the college administration and how to move forward, not knowing how things will turn out.

Case Study Questions

1. How would you advise Biff?
2. Would you recommend that he come clean with the college administration? Why or why not?

Case 21

The Silent Partner

Biff refuses to engage in meaningful conversation with his wife, Mable, often going weeks with only what she calls his "efficiency speech." He speaks to her only to address logistical or practical matters of the home but avoids all intimate interaction, relationship building, and mutual care.

The children appear to cope with their father's limited interaction, but their five-year-old son, Biffy, shows signs of worry and insecurity. Biffy loves his dad but is confused by Biff's cyclic behavior and relational distance. Recently, he asked his mom if his dad was mad at him. Though Mable reassured him, Biffy seemed unconvinced.

Mable reveals that Biff has always struggled with anger, even before they married. His silent treatment has been his primary way of expressing frustration or dissatisfaction. Biff's behavior is deeply hurtful to Mable, who experiences his neglect and dismissiveness. She has described it as a sanitized version of murder, echoing James 4:1-3.

- Physical murder says, "I do not like you, so I am going to make sure you do not exist by killing you."
- Silent treatment says, "I do not like you, so I am going to treat you as though you do not exist by not speaking to you."

Case Study Questions

1. What are your top three questions for Biff?
2. How would you offer hope and help to Mable?
3. What would be your counsel to them regarding Biffy?

Case 22

The Darker Side of the Ministry Mom

Mable has been the go-to person in her church, admired for her dedication to ministry and known for her willingness to serve. Whether counseling, teaching Bible studies, or leading events, Mable is always available and dependable. However, behind the scenes, her home life is far from the ideal picture that her public ministry portrays. Her husband is the stereotypical passive male, having long since disengaged from the marriage struggles, focusing solely on his role as the breadwinner. Their friends were stunned when they witnessed Mable yelling at Biff in the church hallway, revealing a side of her that contrasted starkly with her public persona.

Meanwhile, their teenagers, Biffy and Biffina, are openly rebellious. Though Mable kept them highly active in church activities during the younger years—excelling in Bible drills and looking like role models—their outward appearances masked a deeper dysfunction. Biff's disengagement and Mable's hypocrisy created a fractured home environment, which the children mirrored in attitudes and behaviors.

The family was shaken just before Biffina's seventeenth birthday when they discovered she was pregnant. This revelation caused Mable's carefully constructed world to crumble, forcing her to confront her family's brokenness and the limits of her ministry-driven ambitions.

Case Study Questions

1. How would you counsel this family?
2. How would you re-envision the church about biblical priorities for the home?

Case 23

The Aspiring Counselor Wannabe

Biff, a 42-year-old husband and father, believes the Lord is calling him to pursue a biblical counseling ministry. Seven years into his Christian walk, Biff is zealous about helping others through the transformative power of the gospel. His marriage is stable, and his wife supports his desire to serve. However, both Biff and Mable come from dysfunctional family backgrounds, which continue to influence aspects of their family dynamics.

While Biff's passion for ministry is evident, he humbly acknowledges he is still learning what it means to lead his family well and deepen his faith. He desires guidance on how to prepare for a counseling ministry in a way that honors God and equips him to help others effectively.

Biff has taken the initial steps, such as reading counseling books and seeking advice from mature believers in his church. However, he recognizes areas of needed growth, including deeper theological understanding, consistent spiritual leadership, and addressing lingering patterns from his past. He also wants advice on balancing his ministry preparation with his responsibilities at home, ensuring his calling does not overshadow his commitment to his family or his need to mature. Biff hopes for a clear, practical path to pursue his ministry aspirations while continuing to grow in Christlikeness.

Case Study Questions

1. What encouragement would you give Biff about his desire to serve?
2. What potential concerns would you raise about his readiness?
3. What steps would you recommend for Biff's personal and spiritual preparation?
4. How would you balance affirming his passion with addressing areas that need growth?

Case 24

Meds and More

Three years ago, Biff and Mable became Christians. Biff, 38, and Mable, 39, joined a church shortly after their conversion and began engaging with their community. A year later, Biff expressed his desire to serve on the church's elder board. The church leaders initiated an assessment phase to evaluate his qualifications for leadership.

During this process, the elders became aware of a few challenges in Mable's life. She has a history of treatment with psychotropic drugs for manic outbursts, and she also frequently dominates her small group discussions with her struggles. Group members have expressed their frustration, noting that the meetings often center around Mable rather than serving as a space for mutual edification.

When approached about her behavior, Mable tends to withdraw from the group for weeks. Upon returning, she often presents a new diagnosis, a different label, and a set of medications resulting from ongoing consultations with her psychiatrist. Despite occasional progress, her small group feels impatient due to frequent setbacks.

Mable spends much of her time sleeping, watching television, or surfing the Internet. Meanwhile, Biff juggles his ministry volunteering and family responsibilities as he continues through the eldership assessment process.

Case Study Questions

1. How would you help Biff and Mable?
2. Is Biff qualified to be an elder? Why or why not?
3. What would you tell their small group?

Case 25

The Christian Prostitute

Mable described her marriage in deeply painful terms, saying she feels like a prostitute. She went on to admit that she uses intimacy as a tool to manipulate her husband while he reacts to his unmet desires with pouting or anger. Their relationship is caught in a destructive cycle of sinful behaviors, leaving her feeling hopeless and unsure of how to move forward.

Mable recognizes her contributions to the dysfunction and seeks help to understand her role in the marriage from a biblical perspective. However, she struggles to see a way to break free from the pattern of manipulation and conflict. Biff is unwilling to engage in conversations about their struggles, which adds to her feelings of despair, loneliness, and isolation.

Both claim to be Christians, and there is no reason to dispute their professions. Still, their marriage is marked by mutual self-centeredness, with both spouses focusing on what they want instead of sacrificially serving each other in love. Mable genuinely longs to honor God in their marriage but feels emotionally drained and spiritually disoriented. She desires practical and biblical guidance to navigate her responsibilities and find practical hope for the relationship, even if Biff remains resistant to change, sticking to his business-as-usual mindset.

Case Study Questions

1. How would you counsel Mable to think biblically about her role in the marriage?
2. What would you say to Biff about his sinful attitudes and actions?
3. How would you apply 1 Peter 3:1-6 to Mable's situation?
4. What steps would you guide the couple through if Biff repents?
5. If he remains unrepentant, how would you counsel Mable to glorify God in her marriage?

Case 26

Mable's Search for Self-esteem

Mable, a nineteen-year-old, grew up in a tumultuous home. Her father's instability, expressed through pouting and anger-laced outbursts, created an environment of fear, insecurity, and unpredictability. She vividly recalls curling up in a fetal position at night, listening to her parents argue.

Her mother worked full-time, leaving Mable to rear herself during the day. In her teenage years, Mable sought affirmation through relationships with boys, often turning to promiscuity to fill the void of acceptance and love. Her most recent breakup has left her feeling empty and seeking answers, leading her to counseling.

Mable believes her core struggle is low self-esteem, a belief reinforced by all the self-help books she has been reading. While she became a believer two years ago, her spiritual growth has been stunted due to having no mentor or meaningful connection within her local church. Mable is searching for guidance to understand her struggles and find a path toward true transformation.

Though she feels stuck, Mable's willingness to seek help is an opportunity to address the deeper heart issues driving her patterns and redirect her identity to her worth in Christ rather than the fleeting approval of others.

Case Study Questions

1. Is her problem low self-esteem? Why did you answer the question the way that you did?
2. What is the difference (if any) between low self-esteem and low self-worth? Be clear and specific with your answer.
3. How would you counsel her? Please address the case from at least five different angles, bringing practical care to help her overcome the various issues she needs to consider and change.

Case 27

The Sexually Abused

Biffina, in her 30s, represents many lonely people who have faced the long-term effects of childhood sexual abuse. Biffina, also like so many others, has interpreted her childhood trauma through a lens of self-condemnation. As a result, she now struggles with identity, relationships, and viewing herself biblically.

Despite her faith in Christ, Biffina often feels unworthy, believing lies about her value and her ability to be loved by anyone. Sometimes, these internal struggles lead to strong temptations for someone to love her, leading to compound her problems with bad decisions. It is a combination of Adamic fallenness, the sins of others, and personal moral failure that keeps her in a cycle of hopelessness.

Though she has a limited understanding of the biblical doctrines of sin, salvation, and sanctification, it has not helped. It perversely reinforces her sense of condemnation rather than leading her to the hope found in the gospel. She longs to experience the freedom that only Scripture can provide but feels trapped in a vice of shame and self-doubt.

Biffina's relationships reflect these internal struggles. Fear of rejection and a sense of inadequacy have made it difficult to connect with others. Thus, she seeks counsel to understand her worth in Christ, confront the lies she has believed, and move toward a life that reflects her identity as a child of God.

Case Study Questions

1. How would you affirm Biffina's worth in Christ and confront the lies she believes about herself?
2. How would you explain the doctrine of total depravity in a way that doesn't add to her sense of condemnation?
3. What is Biffina's real identity according to Scripture, and how would you guide her to embrace it?
4. What practical steps would you recommend to help Biffina walk in restoration and freedom?

Case 28

High Standards Tempt Me to Lie

Mable struggles with deep insecurity masked by self-righteousness. Her desire for perfection and a craving for others' approval distort her relationships with both God and those closest to her. Her family is well aware of her tendencies but feels unable to address them because Mable is not humble enough to receive feedback about her faults. In her marriage, Mable's self-righteous attitude often manifests as nagging, criticism, and demeaning speech toward her husband, Biff. While Biff has his struggles, too, Mable's persistent disappointment and a recent ultimatum to leave him if he doesn't change have created a significant strain on their relationship.

During a private counseling session, Biff talked about his frustrations and temptations. He expressed a desire to grow spiritually, describing efforts to change his prayer life, Bible reading, and accountability. However, he admitted feeling overwhelmed by Mable's impossible standards. Her high expectations leave him tempted to lie about his progress to avoid further criticism or conflict. Biff's vulnerability reveals the unhealthy dynamics in their marriage, where grace and patience are overshadowed by fear and pressure. He is seeking guidance on how to reconcile his desire to grow with Mable's demands for perfection and her inability to offer unconditional support.

Case Study Questions

1. Should Biff be completely transparent with Mable? Why did you answer that way?
2. What is your counsel to him?
3. How would you counsel Mable?

Case 29

Confessing Less Than They Know

Biff is seeking counseling after his wife, Mable, discovered inappropriate searches on their home computer. Initially, Biff denied any wrongdoing, claiming ignorance. However, the browser history revealed hundreds of ungodly links, leaving no room for doubt. Since they are the only ones with access to the computer, the responsibility clearly rests on Biff.

After a discussion with their pastor, Biff reluctantly admitted to looking at inappropriate sites but downplayed the frequency, insisting it had only occurred a few times over the past six months. He attributed these slip-ups to work pressures and assured everyone he could control his behavior. What Biff didn't know was that Mable had already discovered his secretive searches two years earlier and stealthily installed accountability software on their home computers.

During counseling, when Biff repeated his minimized version of events, Mable produced a history of reports showing two years of extensive activity. Biff was speechless, unable to deny the overwhelming evidence. At the request of their pastor, Biff and Mable are now seeking counseling to address his problems and the deep fractures in their marriage. Both hope to find a path toward restoration and accountability as they work through these challenges.

Case Study Questions

1. What would be your primary concern about Biff, and how would you work through it?
2. What potential concerns would you have for Mable, and how would you counsel her?
3. Name three possible heart issues that could be going on with Biff. Why did you name these?

Case 30

Present But Not Accounted For

The news of Biff and Mable's teenage daughter's pregnancy sent shockwaves through their local church. In response, the pastors recommended marriage counseling, which you agreed to provide. After four weeks of intensive counseling, several dynamics in their relationship began to surface:

- Biff and Mable's 19-year marriage was essentially an agreement to coexist, though neither of them explicitly acknowledged it.
- Biff, instead of addressing his passivity, chose to escape through work, sports, and pornography. Mable, on the other hand, avoided being a biblical wife by immersing herself in ministry activities.
- Their local church adopted a ministry-driven rather than relationally driven approach, which left them without meaningful support. The church's philosophy was pragmatic and utilitarian, focusing on programs over people.

While Biff and Mable are accountable for how they live, their church bears responsibility for neglecting to provide supplemental care. Hebrews 13:17 reminds us that pastors are responsible for the shepherding and leadership they offer to their people.

The pastor calls you to discuss the counseling process. He asks how the church could have been more proactive in helping Biff and Mable, and seeks your advice on short-term and long-term changes to provide better care for his folks.

Case Study Questions

1. How could the church have been more proactive in helping them?
2. Write out a short-term plan for the pastor to implement.
3. Write out a long-term plan for implementation.

Case 31

Bert, The Flesh Cutter

B iff's friend, Bert, is known for being a practical joker. Bert's sense of humor is a strength that has endeared him to many, but like most strengths, it has become his greatest weakness. Bert rarely allows for serious conversations, leaning heavily on verbal sparring through sarcasm and mocking, which always dominates the conversations. Being with Bert is like a competitive event, often putting others down in front of their peers.

As a ministry leader, Bert's over-the-top communication style becomes a stumbling block. His constant jesting draws attention to himself rather than to the Lord, and his team members are guarded and restrained when he is present. One team member lamented,

> You never know when you're going to get hit with a verbal jab.

Ironically, when Bert is absent, his team becomes more outgoing, thoughtful, and prayerful. Sadly, Bert's behavior has begun to influence others, with many of his friends mimicking his conduct. This environment leaves little room for Christlike encouragement, prayer, or spiritual growth. Biff approaches you for counsel on how to address Bert's behavior. Feeling unequipped because he is "just a church member," Biff struggles with how to confront a leader in a loving yet truthful way.

Case Study Questions

1. What is your theology on the tongue?
2. How would you guide Biff?
3. What are your guidelines about lightheartedness versus seriousness?

Case 32

Counselees and the Local Church

As a Christian counselor working in a parachurch organization, we often receive referrals from local churches to counsel their members. These referrals sometimes reveal troubling dynamics between the counselees and their churches. Here are a few scenarios:

- After contacting a pastor to inform him that one of his members is seeking your counsel, the pastor responds dismissively: "I don't need to know what is going on with them. Fix them and send them back. I'm busy."
- You request that a pastor or leader accompany their church member to counseling for support. The pastor responds: "None of my people are qualified to counsel. Just do it and keep me posted on how it goes."
- You counsel a couple from a church that lacks adequate soul care. The couple realizes their only option for care is to pay for continued counseling or leave their church in search of one that offers better support.

Biff and Mable come to you for counseling. Because they are seeking counseling help outside their church, it raises a potential red flag, suggesting their church may be unable or unwilling to provide meaningful soul care, akin to a patient leaving a hospital to visit an urgent care center.

Case Study Questions

1. How will you navigate through the sticky situations of caring for somebody else's sheep while seeking to lead them back to their local shepherd?
2. When the pastor says he isn't qualified to help, how would you respond to him?
3. How will you walk a couple through the decision to stay or leave a church that does not provide good soul care?

Case 33

Man, Ministry, Marriage

Biff is a popular ministry leader whose love for his work has overshadowed his responsibilities in his marriage and with his children. This dualistic life has led to a fractured family and a dissatisfied wife. For years, Biff has lived a dual life—privately struggling with sin and neglecting his family while publicly portraying himself as a Christlike example to his local church.

Biff acknowledges that he has been using ministry for selfish purposes, rationalizing his actions by muting his conscience through constant busyness. Biff's sanitized sinning allowed him to justify his behavior and avoid addressing the deeper issues in his heart.

Over time, his hardened conscience and dissatisfaction led to more significant private sins, which he rationalized as a safe escape from his struggles. Despite recognizing the need for change, Biff is unwilling to face the possibility of losing his ministry, which has become an idol in his life.

The church leadership is unaware of Biff's struggles, and the congregation continues to see him as an exemplary Christian leader. Meanwhile, his wife's anger grows as she sees the disconnect between his public persona and private failures. Their children, increasingly disillusioned, are distancing themselves from the church.

Case Study Questions

1. How would you communicate hope to Biff's wife?
2. What is Biff's core problem, and why do you think so?
3. What is your detailed plan to help Biff change—assuming he is interested in changing?

Case 34

Mable Marries the Divorced Guy

Mable, a 25-year-old solid Christian, comes from a strong Christian family and is active in her gospel-centered church. She has recently entered a relationship with Biff, a 29-year-old Christian who has been divorced for three years.

Biff became a believer 15 years ago but acknowledges that he hasn't always lived faithfully. At 19, he married Marge, and they had one child together. Despite their shared faith, their marriage was riddled with struggles. Unable to work through their challenges, Biff left Marge and divorced her without biblical grounds.

Since the divorce, Marge has remarried, tying the knot with Bert. Over the last three years, Biff has repented of his sins and committed to walking with God in integrity and humility. His church affirms his character and involvement in ministry and has noticed evident spiritual growth.

Mable and Biff met a year ago, and their relationship quickly deepened. Mable is fully aware of Biff's past, including his unbiblical divorce, but believes that his repentance is genuine. The couple now seeks premarital counseling, desiring biblical wisdom about marriage, divorce, and remarriage. They specifically ask for your position on their situation and guidance on how to move forward in a way that honors God.

Case Study Questions

1. Give your position on Biff marrying Mable.
2. Write a practical plan to walk Biff and Mable through your counseling recommendations. Make as many points as necessary to articulate the various issues you want to cover with them.

Case 35

Past Sex Thoughts in Current Marriage

Biff, a newlywed and a member of your church, comes to you for counseling. His wife, Mable, comes from a family with deep roots in the local church. She grew up attending Christian schools and is now a teacher at the church school. Their relationship was well-known and celebrated within the church community. After two years of courtship, the congregation rejoiced when Biff and Mable announced their engagement and subsequent marriage.

During your counseling session, Biff shared that while Mable remained a virgin until their marriage, he did not. Before coming to faith in Christ about three years ago, Biff lived an immoral lifestyle. However, upon his salvation, he abandoned his sinful behaviors and took intentional steps to lead a pure and God-honoring courtship with Mable. He set clear parameters for their dating relationship and was open with her about his past before their wedding.

Despite his love for Mable, Biff reveals a struggle that has led him to seek your help. When they are intimate, he experiences intrusive images of past sexual relationships. He sees the faces of other women and recalls the things they did together. This ongoing battle deeply disturbs him, and he feels guilt over these memories interfering with their marital intimacy. Biff has not shared these thoughts with Mable as he does not want to hurt or burden her. He desires your counsel on how to overcome these ungodly thought patterns so he can honor his wife and his marriage.

Case Study Questions

1. Is Biff obligated to talk to Mable about his thought life? Why or why not? Depending on your answer, how would you counsel Biff to proceed?
2. How would you counsel Biff about overcoming his thought life?
3. How would you counsel Mable, assuming she learns of what's been happening?

Case 36

She Buried Her Son 10 Years Ago

M able, a 59-year-old Christian woman, comes to you for counseling after enduring decades of profound suffering. Ten years ago, her second son was murdered by his wife, who shot him five times. Despite the brutality of the crime, the wife received only 300 hours of community service. Adding to the anguish are the lies during the trial, and a life insurance payout to the wife's daughter—from a previous marriage—deepened her sense of injustice and betrayal.

Ten years before that tragedy, Mable buried her oldest son, who was also murdered. He had broken into a home, where the homeowner shot him in the head. The police deemed the case unworthy of further investigation, leaving Mable with unresolved anger and frustration.

Now, Mable wrestles with anger, bitterness, and gossip, struggling to reconcile these thoughts with her faith. Her Christianity provides a foundation, but it does not shape her thoughts in ways that bring peace or understanding. Instead, suffering clouds everything, leaving her unable to process her pain through a biblical lens. Mable seeks your help to find a way forward, but her suffering and ongoing anger present significant barriers to experiencing hope and restoration in Christ.

Case Study Questions

1. What would you tell Mable?
2. How would you proceed?
3. How would you help her to guard her heart?
4. What would be your temptations when counseling this lady?

Case 37

I Cannot Connect with My Church

Sylvia has attended a large church in Galveston, TX, for 14 months but feels disconnected despite her efforts and consistent attendance. She has not developed meaningful relationships and struggles to feel part of the community. Her mother, Mrs. Avery, believes that the church's size is the problem and has encouraged Sylvia to consider attending a smaller one. However, Sylvia is uncertain whether her difficulty lies in the size of the church or her hesitancy to engage.

Coupled with the issue that Sylvia has not been totally honest with her mother about all the reasons she senses a disconnect with her church, her husband does not have a problem with it. He is involved with his work and connects well with his teammates on the job. As Sylvia thinks about her husband, their community, and a future family, it only intensifies her desire to settle this problem once and for all.

Sylvia longs to belong to a thriving, gospel-centered community but feels stuck. She recognizes her hesitation to take relational initiative but doesn't know how to overcome the obstacles. She is seeking guidance from you to discern whether she should remain at her current church and work on engaging more intentionally or explore another church where she might feel more naturally at ease.

Case Study Questions

1. How would you help Mrs. Avery think biblically about her daughter's challenge?
2. If Sylvia were seeking counsel, how would you guide her step-by-step in assessing the situation?
3. What role does personal responsibility play in Sylvia's difficulty?
4. How would you replace terms like shy or connecting with biblical categories to describe Sylvia's struggle?
5. What 1970's rock song formed the basis for this case study?

Case 38

The Sinning Victim

Mable recently discovered that her husband, Biff, has been living in adultery for over five years. The shocking revelation came after she found a bar receipt in his wallet, which led to confrontation, further investigation, and confirmation of the affair.

Mable is deeply hurt, angry, and unwilling to forgive. Each time the topic of adultery arises, she breaks down in tears, overwhelmed by the betrayal. Yet, she also humbly acknowledges her pattern of nagging, disrespect, and a lack of encouragement toward Biff throughout their 15-year marriage. While Biff's adultery is a grievous sin for which he bears full responsibility, the broader struggles in their marriage do not arise in isolation.

Biff expresses genuine remorse, a willingness to repent, and a desire to work toward reconciliation. However, Mable remains mostly focused on her role as the victim, unable or unwilling to consider how her sin patterns contributed to the relational dynamics over the years.

As their counselor, you face the delicate and potentially volatile task of addressing Mable's justified hurt and anger while helping her see the need for self-reflection and active repentance. The challenge is to balance compassion for her suffering with a call to evaluate her actions and pursue biblical restoration.

Case Study Questions

1. At what point in the counseling do you bring up her sinfulness in the marriage?
2. How do you walk her through being sinned against versus her guilt that contributed to the adultery?
3. How does the gospel speak specifically and practically to her hurt and her guilt?
4. What do you think is at the core of her self-righteous attitude that motivated her to be a discouragement to her husband?

Case 39

No Thanks for Thanksgiving

This Thanksgiving is a particularly challenging milestone for Biff—it is his first holiday without his wife and children. Earlier this year, his 17-year marriage to Mable ended after years of mediocrity and unresolved conflict. Mable has custody of their three teenage sons, who blame Biff for the divorce.

Biff has been working to rebuild his life, repenting of his contributions to the marriage's failure and re-establishing himself in his local church. While the church community recognizes his efforts, Biff struggles to find his place. He feels disconnected from his old friends, out of place in the singles group, and excluded from the married couples' fellowship.

As Thanksgiving approaches, Biff's loneliness intensifies. He is tempted to exaggerate his struggles to draw attention and sympathy. With most church families engaged in their plans or traveling, no one has invited him to join them for the holiday. Meanwhile, Mable and the boys are heading out of state to spend Thanksgiving with her parents.

Biff reached out to you for encouragement and guidance. He wants you to help him navigate his loneliness and resist the temptations toward self-pity. He also seeks practical advice on forming meaningful connections within his church during this challenging season of transition and isolation.

Case Study Questions

1. What would you tell Biff?
2. How would you help him theologically?
3. What would be your practical advice for Biff?
4. If you have had a similar experience, what would you have liked to have happened to you, or what did others do for you that helped you through your difficult time?
5. If you have not, what would you hope would happen?

Case 40

What About Biff?

Mable has left Biff after 24 years of marriage, citing patterns of ongoing anger, four episodes of physical abuse, mental manipulation, devaluing behavior, and public embarrassment in front of their five children. She also pointed to Biff's unwillingness to seek help as evidence of his lack of desire to change.

In addition to the issues Mable has raised, Biff privately admits to other struggles, including fear of man, hypocrisy, financial debt, pornography, materialism, inordinate desires, sensual thinking, a lack of close friendships, and even toying with adultery. While Mable is aware of some of these problems, her primary concern is the impact of Biff's anger on her and their children.

Biff, professing a desire to reconcile with Mable, seeks counseling. He acknowledges his need for change and expresses regret for how his actions have affected his family. However, his history of inconsistency and highly skilled manipulation leaves Mable skeptical. She has stated that she is not interested in reconciling or counseling with Biff until she sees consistent, practical steps of genuine change. Biff professed faith as a child and attended a conservative church, where he once held the office of deacon, but he has never lived in accordance with his confession of faith.

Case Study Questions

1. Where would you begin with Biff?
2. What would be your advice to Mable?
3. What would be your goals for your first session with Biff?
4. What other information do you need to know from Biff?
5. What is your long-term plan for Biff? What is your long-term strategy for their marriage?
6. What types of homework would you give to Biff, and why would you assign them?

Case 41

When Your Spear Stabs You

Five years ago, Mable and Biff had a whirlwind dating relationship. They were impure, though they rationalized their behavior by marrying hastily. Friends expressed concerns but chose not to intervene, as the couple kept their distance from caring relationships.

Over time, Mable's criticalness and insecurity fed into Biff's desire for respect and affirmation. Four years into their marriage, Biff began a flirtatious relationship with another woman that, within six months, turned into an adulterous relationship. Biff's sins are numerous, and he is fully responsible for his choices. However, through their counseling, Biff admitted and repented of his sins. Today, he is actively walking out repentance, demonstrating humility and life change. Those familiar with his story are inspired by the steps he is taking.

Mable, on the other hand, is not repentant. Her anger, accusations, and divisiveness dominate their relationship. She insists that Biff's adultery is all his fault and refuses to consider how her criticalness and insecurity contributed to the relational dynamic. Her craving for approval created a strain on the marriage, but she remains blind to how these issues have impacted them. No one condones Biff's actions, but it is evident to those involved that the destruction of their marriage has been a shared journey.

Case Study Questions

1. With much detail, how would you counsel Mable?
2. With much detail, how would you counsel Biff?

Case 42

The Troubled Teen

When asked why she sought counseling, Mable explained that her teenage daughter was in rebellion. However, she was caught off guard when the counselor redirected the conversation to the state of their marriage—wondering why he would begin there.

After some reflection, Mable admitted that her twenty-two-year marriage to Biff was marked by dishonor, a lack of respect, and anger issues. These patterns had been present since the early years of her relationship with Biff, and now their family was dealing with the fallout through their daughter's rebellious behavior.

There is a strong and practical correlation between how married couples interact with each other and how their children learn to relate to others. While not every teenage problem is directly caused by parents, the family dynamic often plays a foundational role in shaping a child's attitudes and responses. Mable and Biff's struggles have more than likely influenced their child's current rebellious behavior, making it essential for the parents to evaluate and address their relational dynamics.

The challenge in this situation is to help Mable and Biff recognize their influence on their daughter without enabling the child to view herself solely as a victim of their poor modeling.

Case Study Questions

1. What questions would you ask the mom to draw out her and her husband's role in the child's rebellion?
2. How would you acknowledge the parents' culpability to the child but keep her from thinking she's a victim of her parents' poor modeling?

Case 43

The Addict and His Wife

Biff has battled drug addiction for the past 23 years, repeatedly promising Mable that he would quit. Each time, remorse follows his failures, but his empty assurances have left Mable growing increasingly impatient and disillusioned.

Despite completing six months in rehab, Biff relapsed almost immediately upon returning home. Now seeking counseling, he expresses a desire to restore his family but admits his primary motivation is fear of losing Mable rather than a genuine longing for transformation.

Biff openly acknowledges his addiction and professes a desire to quit, but he is unsure how to achieve lasting change. When the conversation shifts to the gospel as the foundation for sanctification, he struggles to understand its application to his life. While Biff claims to believe in the gospel, he admits confusion about how it connects to breaking his addiction and experiencing true heart change.

Mable, worn out and angry by years of disappointment, is contemplating divorce. She feels trapped in a cycle of broken trust and empty promises. Biff's failure to show meaningful and sustained change has deepened her despair, leaving her uncertain if reconciliation is possible or if she should walk away from their marriage for good.

Case Study Questions

1. Does Mable have grounds for divorce? Explain your answer.
2. Do you believe Biff is a believer? Explain your answer.
3. How could a right understanding and practice of the gospel transform Biff's life?
4. Write out a practical and detailed plan for helping Biff overcome his addiction.

Case 44

Confession of an Imposter's Wife

Mable feels trapped in a marriage where her husband, Biff, has emotionally and relationally checked out. His indifference has tempted her to find self-worth through a series of surrogate husbands, such as achievements, ministry, and activities, none of which have provided the fulfillment she craves.

In an attempt to fill the void, Mable immersed herself in Christian disciplines such as commitment, service, and duty. However, these efforts have left her exhausted and joyless. While she continues to strive outwardly and inwardly, she feels unseen, unheard, and unvalued.

Mable describes Biff as once creative and engaged in their relationship. Now, she views him as self-absorbed, pursuing personal gratification while drifting aimlessly through life. She wants him to fight for her, rescue her, and rediscover the adventurer he used to be. Instead, she sees a man she calls an imposter, disconnected from life and their marriage.

Mable seeks counseling with a desire to see her marriage restored but is unsure how to proceed if Biff chooses to remain unrepentant. She wants to honor God but feels overwhelmed by the relational void and her fading hope for reconciliation. She wonders if there's a way forward for her, even without her husband's engagement.

Case Study Questions

1. How would you counsel the imposter's wife?
2. What is your plan to involve the husband in counseling?
3. How will you counsel the wife if Biff does not repent?

Case 45

No More Fun With Biff and Mable

Mable laments, "This is not what I signed up for," reflecting her deep regret over their 11-year marriage. Their relationship has stagnated, feeling more like two individuals cohabiting than a unified partnership. Biff spends his time at work with his friends while Mable escapes into her routines, often turning to cyber friends on social media for connection.

Though they attend church together, their involvement is superficial, with no one close enough to speak into their lives or hold them accountable. At home, conversations often devolve into arguments unless they watch a movie to distract themselves, keeping them from conflict.

Biff insists that he wants to be with Mable but values the marriage primarily for practical reasons. He appreciates her household contributions, financial support, and physical intimacy. When pressed, he sheepishly admits that her departure would mean losing these conveniences.

Mable says she is trapped in a lifeless marriage. Without biblical grounds for divorce, she believes there is no escape and resents being in a relationship with a man she views as unmotivated to change. Her frustration increases as she wrestles with the tension between honoring her covenant and enduring a relationship devoid of hope or meaningful connection.

Case Study Questions

1. When Mable says, "This is not what I signed up for," what would you tell her?
2. How would you respond to the church in terms of getting them involved in Biff and Mable's lives?
3. What would be your plan to help this couple?

Case 46

Practice Parenting with Adoptive Kids

Biff and Mable adopted Biffina when she was a toddler, bringing her into their family with high hopes and good intentions. Now, years later, Mable has begun referring to Biffina as her "practice child," a term that reflects her frustration and disappointment over Biffina's rebellious behavior. In contrast, Mable describes their biological daughter, Biffette, as easier to parent, further widening the relational gap between the family members.

Biff and Mable are seeking help to understand what went wrong in their parenting and how to address the growing tension in their home. While they recognize that they've made mistakes, they seem unaware of how their attitudes and words have shaped their relationship with Biffina. Both parents feel unequipped to respond to Biffina's rebellion and wonder if her struggles stem from the fact that she is adopted.

Biffina, meanwhile, appears to feel isolated, unseen, and misunderstood, further fueling her rebelliousness. The comparison to Biffette only heightens her sense of rejection and distance. The parents' approach, though well-meaning, has created a dynamic that fails to reflect the gospel's call to love, grace, and unity within the family.

Case Study Questions

1. How would you address Mable's perspective of Biffina as her "practice child"?
2. What heart attitudes would you confront in Biff and Mable, and how would you encourage repentance?
3. What additional information would you want to know to understand their parenting approach better?
4. How would you help them view both daughters through a gospel-centered lens?

Case 47

How Do I Honor My Older Parents?

Mable and Biff have enjoyed a beautiful relationship during their seven years of marriage. They have two children, ages five and two. However, Mable is facing a challenging situation with her mother, who has been pressuring her to spend more time with her during the week. Mable's father is passive, and her mother has always been the dominant figure in the home.

Mable's current responsibilities are overwhelming. She is homeschooling their five-year-old for the first time, which has been difficult as she navigates the organizational and planning demands. Additionally, Biff's long work hours mean their family time is inconsistent, so when he is home, Mable prioritizes being with him. To prepare for that time, she focuses on errands, cleaning, laundry, and other tasks.

Her mother insists that Mable is failing to obey and honor her parents, as Scripture commands. Mable is sensitive to God's will and desires to honor Him, but she feels torn. She doesn't see how she can fulfill her mother's expectations while maintaining her priorities of loving her husband, serving her children, and managing the household.

Mable seeks your advice on how to navigate this dilemma biblically, balancing the commands to honor her parents with her responsibilities as a wife and mother.

Case Study Questions

1. What should honoring her mother look like for Mable?
2. Is Mable sinning by not spending time with her mother?
3. When the Bible says, "Children obey your parents," how does that apply here?
4. How would you counsel Biff and Mable?

Case 48

Bug Off, An Angry Teen

Your friends are deeply distressed about the sudden change in their teenage son's behavior. Once known for his gentle demeanor, he is now withdrawn, frequently angry, and openly disrespectful toward them. Their concern deepens when they discover, after persistent questioning, that their son has been engaging in self-harming behaviors, specifically cutting.

The parents are overwhelmed with fear for his mental, emotional, and spiritual well-being. They are struggling to understand what has caused this shift and are desperate for guidance. Their son has become increasingly resistant to communication, shutting them out whenever they attempt to engage with him about his struggles.

The family dynamic has become tense as the parents wrestle with guilt and uncertainty. They wonder whether their parenting has contributed to the problem and believe they are unprepared to navigate such a serious situation. Their son's refusal to talk, coupled with their fears for his safety, leaves them unsure of how to minister to him effectively.

After the possibility of suicidal thoughts arises, the parents are filled with both panic and urgency. They turn to you for practical and spiritual guidance, longing to help their son but sensing powerlessness to reach him.

Case Study Questions

1. What initial counsel would you offer to the parents to address their fears and focus their thoughts biblically?
2. If the teen refuses to talk, how would you encourage his parents to minister to him?
3. How might the family dynamic contribute to his struggles, and what role should the parents play in addressing this?
4. If the teen threatened suicide, how would you guide the parents practically and spiritually?
5. What other questions would you ask to understand the root of his struggles better?

Conclusion

Congratulations on completing this collection of 48 case studies! These scenarios are not merely fictional examples of real life, but they are tools designed to deepen your understanding of counseling, discipleship, and applying biblical principles to life's messy realities. Whether you are a seasoned counselor, a student in our Mastermind Program, or someone who desires to help others, this case study book is a resource to challenge, equip, and encourage you as you navigate the complexities of soul care.

I encourage you to share these case studies with others. Use them in small group settings, Sunday school classes, or discipleship programs. I intend them to spark problem-solving discussions, sharpen critical thinking, and foster collaborative learning. By discussing these case studies, you can refine your ability to ask the right questions, identify heart issues, and apply the gospel in transformative ways.

Teaching a class with these case studies is an excellent way to engage. Whether you're mentoring a few individuals or leading a larger group, these scenarios provide real-life dynamics to explore and solve together. Walking through the questions as a group creates an interactive environment where participants can learn from one another's insights and perspectives.

If you are not currently part of our Mastermind Program, consider joining. This program offers a structured, in-depth training process to develop your counseling skills further. Learning to counsel biblically is not a quick or easy process—it takes years of study, practice, and humility to grow in proficiency. Our Mastermind Program provides you with the guidance, community, and resources you need to mature into an effective, gospel-centered disciple-maker.

Counseling is not about having all the right answers but walking alongside others as they wrestle with some of life's most challenging situations, always pointing them back to Christ. Remember, counseling is not merely a skill—it's a ministry. It involves patience, perseverance, and a steadfast trust in God's Word. As you work through these case studies and beyond, let them shape you into a vessel God can use to bring hope and help to you and others. The goal is not just to become proficient but to reflect the love, wisdom, and grace of Christ in every interaction.

Thank you for investing your time and effort into this book. As you continue your training and share what you've learned, know that you are part of an ongoing mission to bring the light of the gospel into dark and broken places. May God bless you as you grow in knowledge, maturity, and faithfulness to His calling.

Peace,

Rick

About the Author

 Rick Thomas launched the Life Over Coffee global training network in 2008 to bring hope and help for you and others by creating resources that spark conversations for transformation. His primary responsibilities are resource creation and leadership development, which he does through speaking, writing, podcasting, and educating. In 1990 he earned a BA in Theology and, in 1991, a BS in Education. In 1993, he received his ordination into Christian ministry, and in 2000, he graduated with an MA in Counseling from The Master's University. In 2006, he was recognized as a Fellow of the Association of Certified Biblical Counselors (ACBC).

Other Books Available from Life Over Coffee

Boasting in Weakness
Centering Your Marriage on Christ
Communication
Complete Marriage
Don't Apologize
Exchange the Truth for a Lie
Help My Marriage Has Grown Cold
Identity Crisis
Local Church
Loving Me
Mad
Marriage Devotion We Are One
Politics and Culture
Parenting Devotion from Zero to Adulthood
Sex, Temptation, and Modesty
Storm Hurler
The Cyber Effect
The Talk
Wives Leading
You Decide